Everything I Need to Know I Learned from E.T. the Extra-Terrestrial

Everything I Need
to Know I Learned from
E.T. the Extra-Terrestrial

David Gibson
Illustrations by Amanda Pruitt

Clarkson Potter/Publishers
New York

Introduction

I can still remember very vividly the first time that I saw *E.T. the Extra-Terrestrial* in the theater in 1982. I was only five years old, but I was already obsessed with movies, particularly the swashbuckling adventure films of Steven Spielberg and George Lucas, films that had (and still have!) a permanent hold on my imagination and that of almost *every* child I encountered at the time. *E.T. the Extra-Terrestrial* was an altogether different—but equally compelling—experience. It wasn't loud and fast like many of the films my brother and I would re-create in our suburban backyard. Instead, the film seemed to inhabit a calmer, more emotional space that was just as enthralling and engrossing to my young mind. In fact, there were times when the images on-screen seemed to spill out and into the theater where my family and I sat captivated. The story captured the spirit of my own suburban upbringing so well that it was almost as if I couldn't tell where the film stopped and real life began. I walked out of the theater that day a completely new person. Like so many others, I was transformed by this experience, inspired by the tale of intergalactic friendship and the pure power of cinematic magic that I had witnessed.

I have revisited *E.T. the Extra-Terrestrial* almost every year since its release, and its magic, wonder, and thrills still have a powerful effect on me. Beyond that, I also recognize the ways in which the themes and messages in the film resonate with me and have informed my own values as an adult. The film's emphasis on acceptance, empathy, and showing love to those in need, no matter how different from you they may be, still rings as true today as it ever did. The character of E.T. has been recognized around the globe as a symbol of peace and understanding. E.T. was even adopted as a mascot for the Special Olympics, whose values of friendship, hope, and possibility are reflected in the lessons found in the film.

This book captures the many life lessons found in *E.T. the Extra-Terrestrial*. The film shows us that it is crucial, even as adults, to maintain a sense of wonder about the possibilities of life, love, and friendship.

"E.T. was—and still is—my most personal film."
—Steven Spielberg

CHAPTER ONE

Everyone Needs a Family

Working Together as a Family

In the opening scenes of *E.T. the Extra-Terrestrial*, E.T. and his family work together as a unit to collect and gather plant specimens from the forest of this alien planet. They are so in sync that, upon hearing the hoot of an owl, they all stop their work in unison, their hearts all glowing as they react to the strange noise. At the end of the film, Elliott and his siblings work together in a similar way to ensure E.T.'s safe return to his ship. Families can achieve great things when they work together toward a common goal.

Supporting Your Family

Elliott and his family interact like many other families do. While they may argue, disagree, and upset each other from time to time, they also laugh and play together and support one another when life gets tough. As the family comes closer together, Elliott feels more comfortable and empowered to ask his loved ones for help, including asking his big brother, Michael, to help look for E.T. when he is lost in the forest. It's okay to ask for support from those we love while also offering support when someone, in turn, needs us.

"Mom! Mom! There's something out there! It's in the toolshed! It threw the ball at me."

—Elliott

Finding Your Voice

At first Elliott struggles to be heard by those closest to him. Michael and his friends ignore him, and even his mother, Mary, doesn't believe him when he tells her that he encountered a "goblin." After befriending E.T., Elliott gains confidence and begins to find his voice as a leader, taking charge of the situation to save his extra-terrestrial friend. E.T. also finds his voice in this new world through Elliott and learns simple words and phrases that help him communicate his own needs to his adopted human family. By believing in ourselves, we grow more confident and become empowered to speak up and feel heard.

The Family You Choose

E.T. the Extra-Terrestrial shows us that we can find love and support from a family we choose as much as we can from the family into which we are born. E.T. is drawn to Elliott through the kindness and curiosity he shows and, in the process, E.T. is made to feel part of Elliott's family. The siblings invite E.T. into their lives and learn to love and support him unconditionally. In spite of their many differences, E.T. and the humans who love him connect through shared emotions. We all define "family" in different ways, but ultimately our family includes those who make us feel safe, loved, and supported.

"I never thought of *E.T.* as a science fiction film. I saw this as a story about a family . . . and how E.T. was able to give so much esteem back to Elliott and to Gertie and to Michael and in a sense pull that family together." —Steven Spielberg

"He came to me."

—Elliott

Keeping Your Loved Ones Close

Elliott's father is never seen in the film, but his presence is still felt through the memories that the siblings share after finding his old shirt in the garage. Just smelling his cologne brings back happy memories of trips to the movies and popcorn fights. Similarly, as E.T. leaves to rejoin his family, he reminds Elliott that he'll "be right here," in Elliott's heart. So even when we're physically separated from our family or loved ones, the happy thoughts of them in our minds and the good feelings they stir in our hearts mean they are always close to us.

CHAPTER TWO

Home as a Safe Haven

EARTH...
HOME...
HOME.

—E.T.

Finding Home Away from Home

E.T. and Elliott are both children who have lost a sense of home. E.T. is stranded on a strange planet far from his family, and Elliott is dealing with his own sense of loss following his parents' separation. As their bond deepens, E.T. and Elliott find comfort in each other and discover that, while "home" can be a place, it can also mean a feeling of safety and security you experience with someone close to you. Through closeness with loved ones even outside our immediate biological families, we can discover a sense of home that transcends physical space.

Protecting Your Home

E.T. the Extra-Terrestrial shows us how important it is to protect friends and even the places that provide happiness, comfort, and security. Elliott shelters and protects E.T. from the dangers of the outside world as Mary protects her home and children from the encroaching scientists. With his healing touch, E.T. even provides an especially personal protection to the family he comes to love. These examples illustrate how we can find happiness within a variety of spaces: the planet where we live, the dwelling that we share with our family, and even the body that we each inhabit as an individual. It is important to take care of and protect all of our "homes."

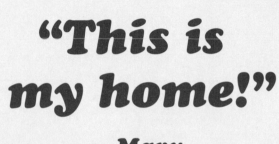

"This is
my home!"

—Mary

How to Cope When Losing Our Sense of Home

Losing a sense of home and security can be a disorienting and painful experience. E.T. is distraught when his family is forced to leave him behind on Earth. Elliott is longing for the comfort of his happy home life and feeling insecure as a result. When Elliott and E.T. find each other, they soon come to see themselves in one another and to rely on each other for compassion as they experience similar feelings. It can help us greatly to seek out others who understand what we are going through. Reaching out to a friend or family member is a good first step toward finding your way "home."

Helping Others Feel at Home

Elliott brings E.T. into his home as a way to comfort him and take away his fear. Elliott provides E.T. with a sanctuary to feel calm and safe, far from the chaos of the outside world and the ever-looming presence of the government scientists. Similarly, Elliott frees the frogs in his science class so they can go back to the forest where they feel secure. These selfless acts illustrate how we can find happiness and love by making others feel comfortable, no matter how different they may be from us.

"When I traveled to different countries for the foreign releases of *E.T.*, my perception of the world changed . . . it seemed everyone was having a profound and heartfelt experience watching the film." —Drew Barrymore

"**YOU COULD BE HAPPY HERE. I COULD TAKE CARE OF YOU. I WOULDN'T LET ANYBODY HURT YOU. WE COULD GROW UP TOGETHER, E.T.**"

—ELLIOTT

CHAPTER THREE

Friendship Is Everything

Sharing What You Love

Elliott and E.T. bond very quickly as friends, and not just because of their shared love of Reese's Pieces! On their first morning together, Elliott proudly and enthusiastically shows off many of his prized possessions to E.T., including his beloved action figures and his pet fish. By sharing the things he loves with his new friend, Elliott opens up to E.T. and allows himself to be vulnerable while also sharing the joy that his toys give him. Sharing things that we value with others allows them to see us, and ultimately love us, for who we truly are.

"THE FISH EAT THE FISH FOOD, AND THE SHARK EATS THE FISH, BUT NOBODY EATS A SHARK."

—ELLIOTT

Embracing Those Who Are Different from You

E.T. and Elliott couldn't be more different on the outside . . . they're not even the same species! All of the children in Elliott's family (including Elliott himself) are scared of E.T. when they first encounter him. Gertie even announces, "I don't like his feet!" as they gather in Elliott's bedroom to uncover the location of E.T.'s home. As the children come to know E.T., they begin to see past his physical appearance and learn that when it comes to friends, it's what's inside that counts most. Elliott and his siblings connect with E.T. emotionally, recognizing that, like them, he is a child who just wants to be home with his whole family. The children see what's in E.T.'s heart (sometimes literally!) and wholeheartedly accept him in spite of their differences.

Making New Friends

After he is abandoned on Earth, E.T. is scared by the strange things he encounters. Elliott is equally scared of E.T. when they first meet by the shed. Elliott eventually finds the courage to reach out to E.T. and to invite him into his home. E.T. accepts this invitation of friendship, which ultimately leads to his rescue. Having the courage to open our hearts to others can lead to truly amazing relationships.

Teaming Up with Friends to Get Things Done

At the end of the film, Michael calls upon his friends Tyler, Steve, and Greg to help with E.T.'s rescue. The boys don't hesitate to gather their bikes for the adventure as Tyler shouts, "Let's do it!" Through the power of teamwork, the friends help E.T. elude capture and get back to his ship. Having the support of a close group of friends can give you the confidence to take on challenges that may seem difficult to face on your own. There is strength in numbers, and with that strength we can accomplish both personal and shared goals.

TYLER: HEY, ELLIOTT, WHERE'S YOUR
GOBLIN? . . .

STEVE: DID HE COME BACK? . . .

ELLIOTT: YEAH, HE CAME BACK. BUT HE'S
NOT A GOBLIN. HE'S A SPACEMAN.

STEVE: AS IN EXTRA-TERRESTRIAL!

CHAPTER FOUR

Be Kind to Others

The Value of Kindness

The kindness that Elliott and E.T. show to each other
affects those around them. Their unique relationship
brings Elliott's family closer together and inspires
Michael and his friends to help Elliott rescue E.T. Even
"Keys," the scientist who is a threatening presence
throughout much of the film, shows kindness and
sympathy to Elliott upon seeing the close bond he
has made with his extra-terrestrial friend. By showing
kindness and compassion, we discover we can influence
others to do the same.

Show Kindness
to All Living Things

Elliott's friendship with E.T. inspires him to open his heart as he recognizes that all living things are deserving of love and safety. When Elliott's science teacher hands out frogs to his class for dissection, Elliott immediately attempts to talk to the frog in his jar, realizing that, much like E.T., the frog is scared and far from home. Elliott leads the class in freeing the frogs, inspiring those around him to engage in a kind and selfless act for the benefit of another living thing. By showing compassion to others, we increase our empathy and can feel more connected to the world.

"I'M GLAD HE MET YOU FIRST."

—MR. KEYS

The Calming Influence
of Kindness

Elliott's home life is slightly chaotic. His family argues at the kitchen table, and his mother is left to parent three children alone in the wake of her divorce. E.T.'s arrival and the kindness he shows to Elliott's family bring an air of calm into the family's home. Even Harvey the dog seems soothed by E.T.'s gentle nature. E.T.'s final, comforting words to Gertie are "Be good." This simple expression is an example of how just a little compassion and kindness can go a long way toward minimizing chaos around—and inside—us.

"(E.T.) was like a guardian angel . . . watching over us and there to teach us about people and a way of life."
—Drew Barrymore

CHAPTER FIVE

Believe in Yourself and Others Will Believe in You

BE GOOD

ELLIOTT:

SWEAR IT ONE MORE TIME.
I HAVE ABSOLUTE—

MICHAEL:

YOU HAVE ABSOLUTE POWER.
YES.

Believe in Yourself

Our first impression of Elliott is of a boy who is on the outside looking in. Michael and his friends ignore him and won't let him join in on their role-playing game. Elliott's own family doesn't believe him when he tells them what he saw in the backyard. Elliott even calls himself "crazy" when he first goes looking for E.T. in the cornfield. But soon his doubts about E.T.'s existence fall away, and Elliott begins to believe in himself as much as he believes his new alien friend is real. He learns to trust his own intuition, ultimately relying on himself to make decisions about how to help his friend. Believing in ourselves is one way to gain confidence and "absolute power" over the decisions we make in our lives.

Inspiring Others with Your Belief in Yourself

Elliott's experiences with E.T. give him the confidence to become a leader, taking charge of situations and rallying the support of those close to him. With his newfound confidence, Elliott inspires his siblings and Michael's friends to help him rescue E.T. and return him to his family. By believing in ourselves, we encourage others to believe in us, too.

Believing in Something
Outside of Yourself

Helping E.T. allows Elliott to take up a cause and to look beyond his own problems long enough to recognize that he is just one small part of a larger universe. Through his relationship with E.T., Elliott learns to believe in something outside of himself and to gain a new perspective on his own life. By finding a meaningful cause to believe in, we can take charge of our lives and gain a sense of greater purpose as we help others.

"(A)ll I can do is make movies that bring space down to Earth and make it more accessible to the imagination."
—Steven Spielberg

CHAPTER SIX

Overcoming Challenges

Solving a Problem

In spite of his brief time on Earth, E.T. quickly adapts and finds unique ways to solve the problems he faces. He hides among the stuffed animals in Elliott's closet so as not to alert Mary to his presence. And when he is faced with the struggle of contacting his distant family, E.T. forms ideas and gathers objects that can help him to communicate. He builds a transmitter, plays with a Speak & Spell, and is inspired by a telephone commercial on TV. All of these experiences inspire E.T.'s imagination, leading him to build the device that will ultimately allow him to "phone home" to his family. By exercising patience, employing our skills of observation, and experimenting with resources at our disposal, we can work to solve any problems we may face.

ELLIOTT: E.T, it's working! It's working!

E.T.: Oh! Home.

Working Toward a Goal

As soon as Elliott discovers that E.T. is an extra-terrestrial from another world, the two friends begin to work toward the goal of getting E.T. reunited with his family and back home. Elliott even recruits his two siblings into their exciting plan as they work together to sneak E.T. out of the house on Halloween by disguising him as Gertie dressed up as a ghost! Through clear communication and creative thinking, the two friends ultimately achieve their goal and grow even closer as they see their plan come to fruition. Planning and working toward a goal allows us to gain agency while working to overcome obstacles in our lives.

ELLIOTT: Okay, now you know
the plans by heart, don't you?

GERTIE: Meet you at the lookout.
At the lookout.

Making a Plan

In order to pull off the thrilling rescue of E.T. from the government scientists, Elliott and Michael concoct an elaborate plan involving a government van, some bikes, and the help of a few good friends. Working together to help their extra-terrestrial friend strengthens Elliott and Michael's relationship as they build and establish trust with each other. Making a plan and seeing it through can help you to feel more organized and clear in your intentions . . . even if your little sister accidentally reveals the details a little too early.

Get Up and Keep Trying

When E.T. first lands on Earth, he's a little wobbly on his feet . . . even before he starts drinking beers out of Elliott's refrigerator! The people, objects, and environments E.T. encounters are strange and sometimes scary, but he perseveres and eventually learns to stand tall thanks to the friendships and connections he makes with the people he meets. By facing things that might at first seem scary, we not only learn to walk tall but we may also even soar across the sky!

Practice Makes Perfect

E.T. the Extra-Terrestrial personifies the value of practice and how it can help one improve in a variety of ways. For example, E.T. practices speaking after learning words from an episode of *Sesame Street* and is eventually able to communicate with Elliott. Similarly, Michael practices backing out of the driveway and eventually his skills on the road (rough as they may be) help rescue E.T. By practicing skills we want to master, we can accomplish anything—and experience fun and adventure in the process!

GERTIE: B. B. Biscuits.

E.T.: Beeeeee.

GERTIE: B! You said B! Good!

E.T.: B. Good.

CHAPTER SEVEN

Dealing with Painful Things

Taking the Pain Away

When Elliott cuts himself on the saw blade, E.T. displays his healing powers, touching Elliott's wound with his glowing finger so the cut magically vanishes. E.T. even tries to heal Michael's "wound" on Halloween night when he misunderstands that the knife going through Michael's head isn't real but is a part of his costume. And through his friendship with Elliott, E.T. also helps him deal with the emotional pain when he has to go home, showing us that we, too, can cope with the painful and scary things in life as long as we have an unconditional friend to count on.

"OUCH."

—E.T.

Finding Strength
in Painful Situations

When Elliott loses E.T. (or at least thinks he does), he experiences heartbreak and pain. The bond between Elliott and E.T. is so strong that Elliott interprets the temporary loss of his friend as a loss of feeling. Still, it is clear that his love for E.T. endures and is amplified into overwhelming joy when he sees E.T. come back to life. Ultimately, that experience gives Elliott the strength to let E.T. go at the end of the film because he knows what's most important is that his friend is happy even if that means they can't be together. We all experience heartbreak, but having unconditional friends means the pain won't last forever, though love will.

"He needs to go home. He's calling his people and I don't know where they are. He needs to go home." —Elliott

"You must be dead
because I don't know how
to feel. I can't feel
anything anymore."

—ELLIOTT

"**I'll Be Right** Here"

A Friend to See You Through Hard Times

E.T. comes into Elliott's life during a time of great emotional distress for Elliott's entire family. In the aftermath of his parents' separation, Elliott and his siblings have had to quickly grow up and band together in many ways to take care of their mother, Mary. E.T.'s arrival allows Elliott and his siblings the brief opportunity to transform their pain into purpose, while also inspiring their imaginations and showing them that their feelings are universal. Helping those we love through difficult experiences brings us closer together and helps us cope with challenges in our own lives.

ELLIOTT: Remember when he used to take us out to the ballgames and take us to the movies, and we'd have popcorn fights?

MICHAEL: We'll do that again, Elliott.

CHAPTER EIGHT

Embrace the Power of Imagination

Our Place in the Universe

The first image we see in *E.T. the Extra-Terrestrial* is a view of the night sky. Throughout the film, the characters gaze skyward, as if seeking hope or salvation from the problems they face on Earth. Elliott looks up to the heavens through his kitchen window after an argument with his family, as if longing to escape, and his love of *Star Wars* and the solar system poster on his bedroom wall show his fascination and sense of wonder about outer space. E.T. uses his powers to levitate balls of clay representing planets in an effort to show Elliott and his siblings where his home truly is. This inspires audiences to feel a sense of curiosity and wonder about our own place in the universe and to expand our perspective on our own lives in an effort to be more open to others/what others are going through.

Believing in Miracles

When the government scientist, known as Keys, describes E.T.'s arrival on Earth to Elliott inside the makeshift medical facility, he refers to it as "a miracle." In some ways, the scientist's cold, clinical examination of E.T. threatens to undermine that miracle. It is Elliott's belief in and love for E.T. that makes E.T.'s heart light glow and brings him back to life. It is important to look for and even expect miracles in your life and to believe in things that your heart can feel, even if they are not easily explained.

"I'll believe in you all my life. Every day. E.T., I love you." —Elliott

Stay Curious

E.T. is an explorer and a collector, as evidenced by the inside of his spaceship, which is filled with exotic plant life that he and his family have gathered throughout their intergalactic travels. Once on Earth, E.T. gazes with wonder at both the towering redwood trees of the forest and the streetlights of Elliott's suburban neighborhood. His natural curiosity about our world and its inhabitants ultimately leads E.T. to Elliott's backyard. Elliott, in turn, is driven by his own curiosity about E.T. when he leaves a trail of candy for his new friend to follow back from the shed. Ultimately, it is their shared curiosity about each other that brings the two friends together. Indulging our curiosity and exploring new experiences can lead to exciting adventures and lasting relationships.

"One night, my dad woke me up and took me out in a field, laid out a picnic blanket, and we stared at a fantastic meteor shower. I saw all those streaks of light moving across the sky, and it gave a jump-start to my fascination with the universe." —Steven Spielberg

The Power of Imagination

E.T.'s mere presence in the lives of the humans he encounters helps to inspire their imaginations and creativity. Even allowing Gertie to dress him up like an old lady shows that E.T. is a willing participant in the act of play. When E.T. is sick, Gertie wishes for him to be okay, inspired by the story of Tinkerbell, who is revived through the power of belief. E.T. even seems to inspire a sense of wonder in Michael's teenage friends when he first appears to them from the back of the government van. His magical presence inspires the boys to take a risk and engage in a thrilling adventure to rescue E.T. that finds them all soaring over their neighborhood on their fleet of bikes. When we look for inspiration and let our imaginations soar, we can find adventure and magical experiences in unlikely places.

ELLIOTT: Only little kids can see him.

GERTIE: Gimme a break.

Mary: Do you believe in fairies?
Say quick that you believe!

Gertie: I do, I do, I do!

Mary: If you believe,
clap your hands.

CHAPTER NINE

Communication Is Key

Communicate Your Needs

For much of the film, both Elliott and E.T. find it difficult to communicate with their families. Elliott's emotional needs are eclipsed by larger problems in his family life, while E.T. is stranded on a strange planet far from his own loved ones. Through his relationship and close emotional connection with E.T., Elliott finds the confidence to open up to his mother and ask for her help when he and E.T. both fall ill. E.T. also learns how to communicate with his adopted human family so that they can better assist him in his plan to "phone home" to his real family on their spaceship. By communicating our needs to the people close to us, we not only feel more connected but we can also accomplish big and exciting things that we may not be able to achieve on our own.

ELLIOTT: E.T. phone home.

GERTIE: He wants to call somebody.

Using Tools of Communication

Without the ability to pick up the phone and call his family, E.T. has to be creative in finding a way to contact them. The clever alien eventually figures out how to build a makeshift but effective communication device from items in Elliott's house after being inspired by a comic strip and a telephone commercial that he sees on TV. Before long, E.T.'s signal reaches his family! Though there are many ways to communicate, sometimes an unconventional approach is needed to really get our message across.

GERTIE: Here he is.

MARY: Here's who?

GERTIE: The man from the moon,
but I think you've killed him already.

Communicating with Nature

Communication with nature and our connection to other living things are important themes in *E.T. the Extra-Terrestrial*. E.T. is very attuned to plant life, as you would expect from an intergalactic botanist, and creates a bond with the geranium that Gertie presents to him, which mirrors his connection to Elliott. The geranium begins to wilt when the two friends become sick together and springs back to life when E.T. makes his miraculous recovery after his family returns to Earth. Elliott himself seems to become more attuned to the natural world after befriending E.T., as he speaks directly to the frog in his science class. Nature even plays a role in the success of E.T.'s transmitter, as the wind and the trees of the forest play an integral role in conducting his signal into space. By interacting and communicating with the natural world, we can feel more connected to the earth and make deep and meaningful connections with all living beings.

Saying More with Less

E.T. only ever learns a handful of English words, but he still effectively communicates his thoughts and emotions to his human friends. Before he leaves Earth, the lovable alien speaks to each of the siblings in small but impactful ways. He reminds Gertie to "be good," expresses his gratitude to Michael by saying, "Thank you," and repeats to Elliott the phrase "I'll be right here" while pointing at Elliott's head, letting him know that, no matter what, E.T. will live in Elliott's heart and mind for the rest of his life. These simple yet heartfelt phrases show that we don't have to communicate volumes to show our feelings. Just a few meaningful and sincere words and expressions are sometimes all it takes.

"I taught him to talk now . . . he can talk now." —Gertie

CHAPTER TEN

It's Okay to Feel Big Feelings

Creating Strong Connections

Many of us—children and adults alike—feel our feelings very deeply. The world can be an overwhelming place at times, but that can also be exciting, particularly when your new best friend is an alien and you've sworn to protect him! E.T. and Elliott's relationship is an example of the kind of close connection that we make with friends who are safe and reliable. As their friendship grows, E.T. and Elliott both count on each other for help and support. Elliott provides E.T. with a safe, homey environment from which to hide from the government agents, and E.T. inspires Elliott to have confidence leading his daring rescue—and, perhaps even more daring, to give his school crush a kiss! In the process, the two friends create a strong bond. It is important to reach out and make connections to others—it's how we find the kind of friends who truly understand us and what we may be going through.

Overcoming Fear and Sadness

E.T. the Extra-Terrestrial shows us that it's okay to express ourselves, including in sad or scary times. E.T. is frequently overwhelmed and frightened by the things he encounters on Earth, whether it be a screaming Gertie, a barking Harvey, or an exploding umbrella! Still, Elliott's assurance that he'll "be right here" helps E.T. understand that he won't have to weather these feelings alone. When E.T. and Elliott finally part, they are both heartbroken to leave each other, but E.T. reminds Elliott that he, too, will "be right here." We don't have to deal with feelings of fear and sadness alone since the people who truly love and care for us are always "right here."

Feeling Each Other's Feelings

As their relationship grows, E.T. and Elliott begin to form an unbreakable bond, eventually literally feeling each other's emotions and even becoming ill together close to the end of the film. Elliott begins to speak about E.T. as if they are one and the same. Through this close relationship, we are inspired to have empathy and to be aware of others' feelings. By putting ourselves in someone else's shoes, we come to a better understanding of the needs of others. We share our world (and possibly even the universe!) with so many living things that it benefits us all to deepen our compassion in order to make the universe a place we all can happily inhabit.

"There's a lot of my life in the film . . . I intended the film to reflect the feelings I had as a kid."
—Steven Spielberg

Dealing with Big Emotions

In the film's most famous scene, Elliott and E.T. soar over the forest and past the large full moon on Elliott's bike, powered by E.T.'s telekinetic abilities. Elliott is terrified as the bike careens toward the cliff, then ecstatic as he and his friend take flight. In this scene, E.T. is really "carrying" Elliott, allowing him to start letting go of his fears and to experience the joy of living and the wonders of being a kid. After that thrilling experience, Elliott is inspired to take control of his own life—from opening up to the rest of his family, leaning on them during tough times, and sharing more of himself. Through the power of friendship and imagination, just like E.T. and Elliott, we, too, can soar, enjoying the thrills, wonder, and magic of whatever life brings us!

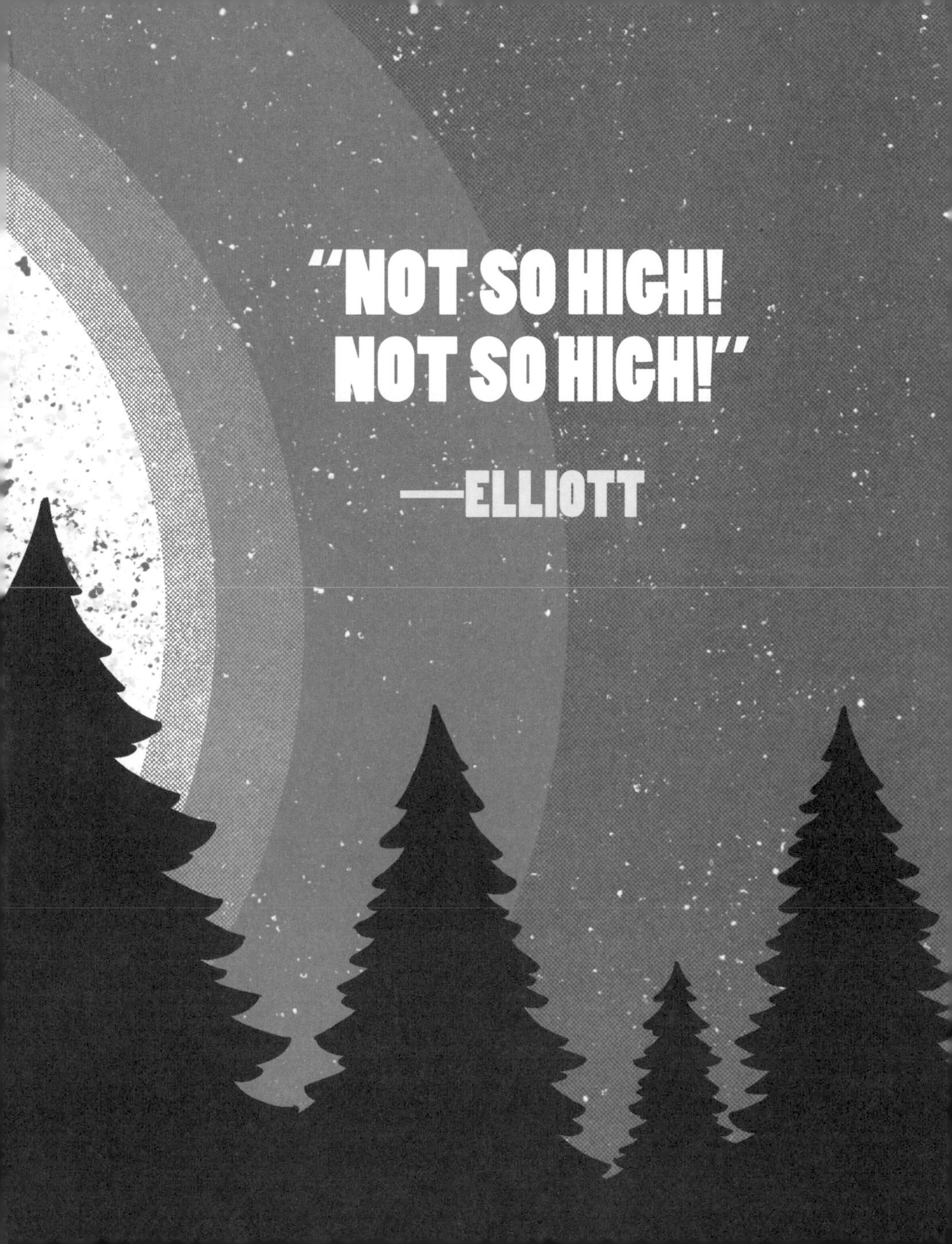
"NOT SO HIGH!
NOT SO HIGH!"
—ELLIOTT

Copyright © 2022 Universal City Studios LLC. All rights reserved.

Published in the United States by Clarkson Potter/Publishers, an imprint
of Random House, a division of Penguin Random House LLC, New York.
ClarksonPotter.com
RandomHouseBooks.com

CLARKSON POTTER is a trademark and POTTER with colophon is a
registered trademark of Penguin Random House LLC.

Library of Congress Cataloging-in-Publication Data is available upon
request.

ISBN 978-0-593-23404-4
Ebook ISBN 978-0-593-23405-1

Printed in China

Editor: Sahara Clement
Designer: Lise Sukhu
Production Editor: Abby Oladipo
Production Manager: Jessica Heim
Copyeditor: Andrea Peabbles
Compositor: dix!

10 9 8 7 6 5 4 3 2 1

First Edition